I0202519

The
CUPCAKE

2017 POETRY COLLECTION

by Eric Nixon

Cover image and design by Eric Nixon.

© 2018 by Eric Nixon

ISBN-13: 978-0-9984362-2-7
ISBN-10: 0-9984362-2-4
BISAC: Poetry / American / General

All rights reserved. No part of this book may be copied, reproduced, stored in a retrieval system, or transmitted in any form or by any process without first obtaining written permission from the author; the exception being a reviewer who may quote brief passages with appropriate credit.

That being said, I'm pretty flexible with fully credited adaptations. Please contact me if you are considering adapting or remixing any works contained within this book.

All situations depicted in this book are products of the author's imagination and may not match any reality known to otherwise exist elsewhere.

Published by Double Yolk Press in Galena, Illinois.
EricNixonAuthor@gmail.com
EricNixon.net

DEDICATION

For Wendy.

Your gift of the cupcake was the wake up call from the Universe I needed to finally get going and focus my energy on my creative career. Thank you.

AUTHOR'S FOREWARD

News-wise, 2017 was a terrible year. Personally, it was interesting. I left my twenty (plus)-year career as an award-winning hotel General Manager and moved from Portland, Oregon to a tiny rural Illinois town to spend my time focused solely on writing. In regards to life-changing choices, that was a big cliff to jump off of.

As scary as it was, it worked. I was able to *finally* finish and publish my science fiction novel, *2492: Attack Of The Ancient Cyborg*, which I've been writing for the past thirty years. For me, this was huge, huge, *huge* and seeing the finished book sitting on my desk makes me radiate with joy.

Earlier in the year, I was afraid that I was writing so little that I would not have enough material to publish a book of poetry for 2017. That changed quickly after moving and I began to write poems at a fast rate. Looking back through what I've written, I'm very proud of this collection and I think it's my best. I hope you agree.

Please enjoy and thank you!

Eric

TABLE OF CONTENTS

Neverdones
Full Moon Skylight
I Fear For The Future
Book World
Writing Instead Of Choring
1,000
I Saw Your Contrail
Wide Load
The Dusty Remnants
Wallet Your Ripple
Their Peephole Worldview
If Gratitude Were A Color
Egg And Cheese, No Meat
Patriotism Is Not
$10,000
The Generous Dumpster

December – 15 poems
Normalcy
Watering Down
Despicable Diners
Think Outside The Tree
Knowing The Potential
Suitcases Of Beer
Just Like That
The Land Is Quiet
I Wouldn't Understand
Powdered Sugar
Window Shopping
In Flyover Country
A Cold So Deep
I Am Not Concerned
Squeaky Crunching

2017 total: 115

JANUARY

The Time Span At Hand

The last one is done
The new one is here
Time to put the past
Back where it belongs
And focus our energy
On the time span at hand

> January 1, 2017
> Portland, Oregon

Bully Ballet

The day after the historic snowstorm
In an area that doesn't know how to deal
With such a deluge of the white stuff
I watched as the bully ballet unfolded
At the empty snow-covered parking lot
The one that used to be a K-Mart
And now has been hermit-crabbed
By some Christian-ish kind of church.
Big-boy trucks with names like
RAM and F-250 raced, spun, and slid
Across the ice and through the snow
Occasionally narrowly missing
A light pole or one another
No doubt hootin' and hollerin'
As they jammed the brakes
And slammed the steering wheel
Showing their dominance
Over what nature changed
Their short-term reality into.
It's not muddin', but it'll do.

> January 11, 2017
> Vancouver, Washington

I know a few years ago I wrote a poem called "Rural Ballet" but
it's ok. I think I can safely appropriate words, phrases, and images
from myself. Anyway, it really did look like some chaotic ballet
performance with those trucks zooming across and spinning
through that huge parking lot.

Prudent Practicing

The day after the historic snowstorm
In an area that doesn't know how to deal
With such a deluge of the shite stuff
I watched the prudent practicing
At the empty snow-covered parking lot
The one that used to be a K-Mart
And now has been hermit-crabbed
By some Christian-ish kind of church.
A small collection of trucks gathered
To use the open space and rare conditions
To safely practice winter weather driving
Putting themselves into terrifying skids
And working through how to handle it
Over and over, getting better and better.

January 11, 2017
Vancouver, Washington

While I strongly suspect the intentions of the drivers were more along the lines of the previous "Bully Ballet" poem, I wanted to envision a different, more positive, side of what I witnessed. I just thought it would be interesting to work this version out.

January

The Cupcake

FEBRUARY

A Question

"Ya wanna know what?"
Is a question
No one ever
Wants to know
The answer to
But we all know
They're going
To tell us anyway
Whether or not
We want to hear it

February 1, 2017
Vancouver, Washington

Not So Smart

Driving across the multi-lane bridge
An off-shoot of an interstate
Where the traffic is flowing fine
Until the little blue and white blur
Weaved its way cutting through
And cutting off cars and trucks
A Smart car with a not so smart driver
As it narrowly missed the front bumper
Of the big-rig semi by an arm span
Seemingly oblivious of its presence
Swinging into the left lane
Only to make its way back right
Half a minute later and continued
Its death-wish driving until it was
Somewhere ahead and out of sight

February 5, 2017
Portland, Oregon

Seriously, when you're driving a car that's barely bigger than a shopping cart, you really shouldn't be blindly cutting off tractor-trailer trucks.

We Expect

We expect mild embellishment
From the advertisements
That companies release
Regarding their products
And what they can do for you
We expect doublespeak
From our politicians
Who can never give a clear
"Yes" or "No" answer to anything
We expect the truth
From our President
The one person representing
You, me, and our country
On the world stage -
A place where,
If things continue in this way,
We expect we will not be allowed to return
Until we learn some basic manners

February 5, 2017
Portland, Oregon

Too Much

My Facebook is blowing up
With alerts topped with
Outraged comments
From my friends
Who can't believe the latest
Horrible thing he's said or done
Issuing proclamations
Without the slightest regard
For what's constitutional or not
News blasts from NPR or the BBC
Reporting on the same things
Or from an Internet celebrity
Adding their two cents to the topic
All of this multiplied
By every social media outlet
I normally let my eyes see
Is just too overwhelming
Is just too much
For me to handle
And I need a break from all of this
Because the ruination of America
Used to be a more manageable
Easily digestible slow and steady decline
Not a flaming dumpster fire falling off a cliff

February 5, 2017
Portland, Oregon

In What Country

In what world
Are double standards
Perfectly permissible?
In what continent
Are cheaters and liars
Rewarded and not punished?
In what country
Is the obvious truth
Freely scorned and ignored?

This one.

>   February 5, 2017
>   Portland, Oregon

Tryant

Trying
So hard to be
A tyrant
Rebranding
Reinventing
Yourself
Into a "tryant"
Working overtime
Purposely aligning
Your image to make
It appear you're terrible
Because that's what you
So desperately want to be
And you won't stop until
You make each and every
Person out there love you
Which is so hard to do
Because in reality
You're actually
So very hugely
Insignificant
Like an
Ant

February 5, 2017
Portland, Oregon

Once I saw this was forming a shape, I could not stop.

You Can Tell By The Glow Reflecting

Watching the moon tease its way
Through the thick
Stacked layers, the
Darkening shades of the
Swiftly moving
Billowy clouds
The full roundness never shows itself
Not completely
Leaving the mind
Wondering what
Is being hidden
Is it on purpose
Or is it coincidental?
I don't think so
You can tell by the glow reflecting
That this thing
Is meant to be seen
Is meaning to entice
Is there for a reason
And the clouds
Which you assume are incidental
Are actually co-conspirators
And a co-dependent player
In this whole situation
Casting a shadow
On all you know
All the while
Setting the stage for what's to come

February 10, 2017
Portland, Oregon

A few minutes ago, I looked out the kitchen window and saw the eerie glow of the full moon on the multi-layered, swiftly-moving clouds. As the clouds shifted, it revealed brief glimpses of the moon without fully showing it. Kind of like nature's strip tease.

That visual, combined with K. Flay's song, "Blood In The Cut" on repeat helped to bring about this poem.

I Need Space With This

I need space with this
Move the rest down
And out of sight
To give me
The clear mind
And the mental blinders
I need to get this done

February 10, 2017
Portland, Oregon

While writing "You Can Tell By The Glow Reflecting," I was getting distracted by the other chunks of lines in my Line Ideas document, so I thought, "I need space with this," and inserted a page break to give me a blank page. I listened to "Good Morning" by The Dandy Warhols, which set a good mood for this

The Songs I Used To Hate

It's funny how
The songs I used to hate
The songs I always skipped
The songs I could never stand
Are the same ones
I find myself
Strangely
Really liking
Or
Discovering their brilliance
The melodies, the music,
Once lost on me as a youth
Now found their way into my head
And repeating on my playlists
From now on

February 10, 2017
Portland, Oregon

The song that specifically brought this line of thinking about today was "Dreams" by Fleetwood Mac (I think?). I only know the Letters To Cleo version of the song. The first time I heard it I was like, "Ugh. That's a cover of some crappy song from the 70s." Somehow that cover version ended up on my iPod playlist I listen to every day at work. It has about 1,200 songs on it, so I go weeks or months without hearing the same song twice. Anyway, that "Dreams" song came on and I actually found myself liking it. Later that day, I heard the original song on the radio. I much prefer Letters To Cleo's version, but it got me thinking.

Kari has always gotten mad at me for not knowing original songs, only the cover versions. Growing up, my family never listened to "popular" music of the 70s and 80s. My father only listened to music in the car, and even then it was only "oldies" from the 50s and 60s. My mom had a few cassette tapes of stuff like Richard Clayderman, Barry Manilow, and Kitaro and would only listen to it

27

privately on a Walkman. That left my only musical influences being whatever my older brother brought home, or what I discovered on MTV (back when they actually played music videos).

I would like to think I'm getting better about music and being open to new things. My main tastes are heading into the indie non-vocal world of bands like The American Dollar and El Ten Eleven (which I find perfect for listening to while focusing on manifesting my future and meditating on spirituality), while also branching into "new-to-me" groups like The Rolling Stones.

February

The Cupcake

MARCH

The Cupcake

A few weeks ago
My boss flew in
To give me my annual review
Something I was expecting
To go swimmingly
Since I was so extraordinary
In so many ways
Such as:
Winning the most prestigious award
My continental-spanning hotel company
Bestows on the best of its best hotels,
An award I've chased for the entirety
Of my twenty-two years in this industry,
I also had the highest guest satisfaction scores
Out of all of our corporately-managed hotels,
And being the best in several other ways,
However
I just barely missed the revenue goal
By two one-hundred-thousandths of a percent,
I missed another goal by less than one percent,
And another by two percent
But all-in-all, I had an astounding year
Being the consistent source of praise
For my boss, her boss, and the entire brand
So, when she flew in for my review
I was pumped up and ready
Excited for the great review
I expected to match my year

When she arrived in my office
She set a small box on my desk
Before dialing in her boss
On speakerphone
To join in my review.
With him on, she said
How she likes visual aids
And opened the box

To reveal a beautiful cupcake
Expertly decorated
With a frosting flower
That was intricate
And delicate enough
To look like
It was made by nature
And not a baker
She told me this cupcake
Represented my hotel
And my management of it
In 2016

My head tilted
As I tried to think
Of where this was going

She went on to say
That outwardly
I had an amazing year
I won the Torchbearer Award,
I was the best in the entire company
With two of our ten
"Winning Metrics,"
I did this, that, and this other thing
Better than anyone else
That, yes, 2016 was a great year
For me and my hotel

"*But...*"

This is when she asked me
To "pick up the cupcake"
Which is when I finally realized
Where this was going
And what she was doing

I glanced up
At her squinched-up face

The Cupcake

Frozen in a self-proud grin
Like Headmistress Umbridge
In a Harry Potter book
Eager to inflict
A painful punishment
As she stared in hungry anticipation
At the cupcake
My hand was slowly reaching toward
All the while my mind was shouting
"No! This is a trap!"
But it was one I had to spring
To release the carefully planned theater
She spent all day concocting

I grabbed
I lifted
And to no surprise
The top of the cupcake
Came off in my hand
Revealing the cake portion
Which had been hollowed out
And looked as if
The core had been removed
With a melon-baller, or a spoon,
Leaving the paper wrapper part
Holding in a thin ring
Of chocolate cake
And nothing else

The look of pure glee
Spread across her face
Like some sort of Dursley Teletubby
Clapping and shouting,
"Again! Again!"
At an act of terrorism
Destroying something she hated

She said that while outwardly
I appeared to have a great year

March

It was really just empty inside
Because the profit I gave them
Wasn't as much as they expected

So what she was saying was that
All of the success we achieved
All of the struggle we slogged through
All of the awards we earned
All of the battles we fought
All of the charts we topped
All of the sweat we bled
All of everything in 2016
Was just pretty window-dressing
But in the end, it was empty.
It was all for nothing.

She began to drone on
About how, "Next year,"
I could really be great
And how, "Next year,"
I could be the best…
…that's when I stopped paying attention
As her words faded into the background
And I fought the urge to stand up,
Lean forward, and smush the top portion
Into her smug mug prattling on
Like an insufferable know-it-all,
But what did rise was the anger
At her saying this pretty, hollow cupcake
Represented the efforts of my past year,
Symbolized the hard work of my staff,
And characterized the summation of my career.

She then went into length
About how
The cupcake
Came to be:
She went to a local bakery
Picked the prettiest cupcake

And asked for it to be
Hollowed out
By the confused staff.
As she regaled the story to me
How she explained to them,
The strangers at the bakery,
What she wanted them to do
The point she was driving home
And why she felt I deserved this.
She then asked what I thought of it.

I was put in a position
Where I had to stifle my emotions;
She's my boss
And her boss
Was hanging on our words
While listening in on speakerphone
I found myself surrounded
And thought it best to play nice
To get past this analogy in chocolate
Sitting in front of me
So I told her that this was,
"Really something,"
And that, "I'll never forget it,"
None of which were lies

After she left
And was safely in another state,
She sent me my review
In the human resources online system
Which scored me in a range
Better fit for someone
Who didn't give a shit
Overlooking my numerous successes
And labeled me as *needs improvement*
In every category I could be rated on,
Which I expected to be in the range
Of *above average* to *exceeds expectations*
Her callous disregard

Stung my eyes and enraged me
As this woman
I had only met twice before
Flung the low numbers like knives
Each one hitting me hard
Stabbing through the love I had for my career
Wounding my motivation
Bleeding out my enthusiasm
Killing my desire to work
For this company
I had spent the bulk
Of my career with
For this company
I personally identified with

No.

I spent the weekend nursing my wounds
Telling myself that I did a great job
And reviewed the actual data and numbers
Which backed up, and then some,
The *phenomenal* job our hotel did
I stifled the indignation and quieted my mind
And tried to focus my energy
So I did what comes naturally to me:

I wrote.

I went into the HR system
Opened my review
Clicked on the *Leave A Comment* box
And I wrote
The longest goddamn reply
To an annual performance review
Anyone has ever written
Where I disputed, argued, and presented
Pages of facts, figures, numbers, and quotes
Many taken from their own emails to me
And when I finally finished and submitted it

I once again felt great about myself
And the job I did

From that day onward
I went about my job
In the same perfect manner
Just as I always did
And played the happy guy
With a smile on my face
Which was noticeably bigger
Since now it concealed a secret:
From the moment
The cupcake
Landed like a bomb on my desk
I began to actively plan
My escape from corporate *life*;
A brow-beaten existence
Where superiors seriously believe
They can motivate good employees
And make them work harder
By knocking them down

The plans are in motion
And before the end of the year
I will shock them
By doing the unexpected,
Resigning and moving;
Walking away from
My decades-long career
And starting something new.
I don't care about sending them a message
Or telling them the reason why
Because I no longer care
They took that from me
So I took my awesome self
And my expertise from them
Leaving me better off
And them without the rock
They had relied on for so long

March

In the end, thanks to the cupcake,
I'll be much happier
Following my life's purpose
Instead wearing myself out
Chasing their numbers

Speaking of the cupcake
As pretty as it was
It was flavorless, dry, and gross
So I threw it away

March 12, 2017
Portland, Oregon

As far as I know, they didn't even read my comment on my review because no one mentioned it.

Less than three months after writing this, I left.

While I wrote this poem, I listened to two songs on repeat, "The Beautiful People" by Marilyn Manson (for the first three-quarters of the poem) and "Tennessee" by Arrested Development (for the latter portions).

APRIL

Pay It Forward Drive Thru

While on a trip to the Midwest
I stopped at a beloved donut chain
I haven't been to in the past four years
And placed my order at the drive thru
I waited my turn and pulled up to the window
Where the young woman shot me
A rehearsed smug smile and informed me
That the person ahead of me paid my bill
And asked if I wanted to "pay it forward"
To the car behind me
The expression on her face
Told me that she had some sort of vested interest
In the continued success of this social experiment
That I suspected her pastor,
Or some other churchly official,
Put her up to
I also thought the term "pay it forward"
Was completely inaccurate in this case
As everyone was actually "paying it backward"
To the car behind them
She sensed my hesitation
And asked if I wanted to know
The bill of the car behind me
I clearly said yes
And found it was a few bucks more
Than what I was supposed to spend
Than what I wanted to spend
So I said no
And the drive thru person
Acted like I slapped her
Saying, "Are you *sure?*"
Pressed by the position
Of holding up the line
I ended up relenting
Ugh, *whatever*
It was only a few bucks
So I surrendered and paid for the car behind me

April

And then waited for another eight minutes for my food
Because all of this "paying it forward"
Screwed up their ordering system
And they lost my order

Lesson learned

      April 15, 2017
      Dubuque, Iowa

During that entire exchange I felt like Larry David on *Curb Your Enthusiasm*

Midwestern Real Estate Bingo

Having spent untold hours
Looking at home listings
In the Midwest
More than a few similarities
Have clearly emerged
Making a new and fun game
Of Midwestern Real Estate Bingo.
Claim that space if you happen to see:
- An oversized clock
- A built-in kitchen desk
- A basement bar
- Bossy words of some kind
  telling you to "Relax,"
  "Welcome," "Breathe,"
  or, "Live, Love, Laugh"
- And the sectional couch
  Curving around the room
  Enticing and enchanting you
  With the cup holder armrests
Chances are that you'll get
More than one of the above
On the very first house
Whose listing you look at
Because that's how
The Midwest rolls

April 16, 2017
Galena, Illinois

Seriously. Every frickin' house.

Record Store Day

Today, on Record Store Day
A man standing in the line
Somewhere near behind me
Said on his phone,
"This is insane!"
I looked around to see
If we were seeing the same thing
And saw only the orderly line
Full of polite people
Patiently waiting
A few were quietly talking
But most were silent
Contradicting the insanity
This embellisher was describing
Which didn't go far enough
So, in his excited state,
He continued to exaggerate,
"Seriously, it's a madhouse!"

Huh.

April 22, 2017
Portland, Oregon

Maybe if he said, "This orderly and polite line is longer than expected!" then I wouldn't have needed to write this.

MAY

The Starer

At Subway
Just after the lunch rush
I sat down at a table
With my freshly-made food
Delishing away in front of me
But there, in the booth beyond,
Sat the starer
A guy in a plain black t-shirt
Intently eyeing the room
In a way that doesn't feel right
Like the full compliment
Of social mores was never loaded
Into his consciousness
And now because of the seat I chose
I'm facing him
So I'm focusing on my food
But
At the edges of my awareness
I sense the heat of his intensity
Like the Eye Of Sauron
Staring at me
For…
Way…
Longer…
Than…
Necessary…
Before the beam of his gaze
Shifted elsewhere
To one of the other few patrons
Unlucky enough to be here now
Again, I would not look up
Full into his eyes
Purposely denying him
Of any kind of connection
Which is what he is craving
The hungry, predatory kind
That no one ever wants

To feel falling on them
I dare to raise my view
Enough to see his table
Empty and lunchless
A cell phone sitting unused
A cell phone, which could have
Diffused and diminished
The creepiness factor
By a hundred fold
If he had only stared at it
Like normal people
Instead of staring at the rest of us
As if he were trying to corrupt our very souls

May 26, 2017
Vancouver, Washington

This completely normal looking guy was super sketchy not just staring at me, but *everyone* in that Subway for a solid 20 minutes before he got up and left.

Staring at your phone = normal and completely accepted.
Staring at people around you = wicked creepy.

Framing

Taking and
Framing
Something old
And familiar
With a fresh
Coat of paint
So that now
Wearing
A fresh look
Around the edges
Makes the accustomed
Into something new

May 28, 2017
Portland, Oregon

Holding It In

A true test of
Mind over matter is
The will of myself
Versus the pressure
Of my pleading bladder

May 28, 2017
Portland, Oregon

I'm not sure when I wrote this silly little thing, but it was in my notes so I'm putting it here without further comment.

JULY

Purse Guarded

In a nice breakfast restaurant
Located in a picturesque
Historic Midwest town
Sat an older woman
Dining with her husband
But what caught my eye
Had nothing to do with her
But rather what she was doing
As she sat with her ordinary-looking
Purse guarded firmly in her lap
Hands on the table
Forearms folded downward
Like wings protecting
Boxing in the bag
As her elbows nearly touched her legs
I looked around
At nothing out of the ordinary
Just other people enjoying
Eggs and pancakes
At this early hour
Where robbery
Is especially unlikely
But there she was
Trying to hide this thing
With her entire body
Implying whatever it contained
Was worth more than her life
Which made me curious
As to the contents
What could possibly be worth that much?
A better person would do the world a favor
And find out
But as for me, my breakfast arrived
And I no longer cared
About the momentary mystery
Of oddity that captured my attention

July 3, 2017
Galena, Illinois

True story that happened at the Golden Egg Café.

Conversational Shift

Walking around our new touristy town
As we were checking out some of the shops
The proprietors naturally struck up conversations
Telling us about tours we could take
Or special deals that were just for the day
And when they naturally asked where we were from
And we said we just moved here last week
We felt the conversational shift
As they went from treating us like the tourists
Thronging around in every direction
To talking to us like new neighbors
And offering wisdom and advice

        July 3, 2017
        Galena, Illinois

Clouded Together

The light of the Moon
Illuminating the cracks in the clouds
Showing the spaces
Between space and here
The weakened spots
Where the light spills out
Highlighting the texture
And the detailed work
Of the condensing water vapor
Showoffing the splendor,
The contrasting fragments
Clouded together
Arranged chaotically
But beautifully
As if nature were creating
A living, moving painting
Just for me
And my two little dogs
Peeing in the grass

July 8, 2017
Galena, Illinois

I just want to clarify: the dogs were peeing, not me. Also, I wrote this while listening to Grizzly Bear's song "Sleeping Ute."

Perfect Day

Today is a perfect day
Not from anything
I have seen or observed
But rather
Because everyone
Keeps telling me it is

> July 9, 2017
> Galena, Illinois

In our descendant society, repetition of a belief apparently makes it true.

Wantrepreneur

The person who sees others' success
And craves it desperately
Needs to experience it
And is more than willing
To fake it until they make it
Only they don't ever get
To that second step
Just keep hitting the faking part
On repeat for years
Doing whatever it takes
To swim in the same circles
As their prosperous heroes
Tagging everything
In a specific way
Trying to attract the attention
Of their unbeknownst mentors
An indifferent "like" thrown their way
Would be the difference between
"Making it" and "Failure"
To the wantrepreneur
Who seems incapable
Of making their own success
Instead spends their time and life
Replicating, repeating,
Mimicking, glomming
Onto the coattails of someone
ANYONE
With the magic formula
The social media presence,
The followers, and the lifestyle
They imagine for themselves
In their own outclassed way

July 9, 2017
Galena, Illinois

The Cupcake

Yesterday, I heard a friend use the word "wantrepreneur" and it burned bright in my mind as being so goddamned descriptively perfect of so many people I've seen online.

A Torrent Of Torment

I already knew
This country would be difficult
When I chose to come here
But the current rush of overflow
The opening of the floodgates
From Lake Stupidity
And Ignorance River
Have created a torrent of torment
Unlike anything ever seen
Where the twin bedrocks
Of science and progress
Are being eroded
To dangerous new standards
Unable to support anything
Stable or safe
Or anything resembling
What we're used to
As each ideal
And pillar of identity
Is abandoned enthusiastically
In favor of hypocritical doublespeak
Set to thunderous applause
And desperate flag waiving
As the land we stand on
Becomes more porous
And holey every day
As it looks like pretty soon
Everything will collapse
From the sheer weight of contradiction
Tidaling toward us
All we can do is brace for impact
And hope to survive
So we can clean up this mess
And start it all over again

July 9, 2017
Galena, Illinois

In the past I've always been shy to write poetry reflecting the political climate. Over the years, I've deleted hundreds of poems I wrote that had a political tinge to them. It's different now. I don't see any way to just let this one go; the stakes are too high this time. Thinking back ten years, it now seems quaint and childish to be upset about previous variations of our government. It's like things have been escalated to absolutely absurd levels and to sit idly by and hope to wait things out is irresponsible. As a society we need to shine the brightest light upon and point out injustices otherwise we could easily find ourselves subjected to something sinisterly incompatible with the freedom we enjoy in this country.

July

The Cupcake

AUGUST

Tethered To The Memories

Depending on who you ask
The decline started about when
We moved to the city
Or some years before then
Either way we saw it first-hand
As the Portland I was entranced with
Where intrigue and wonderment
Found in the surprisingly original details
Several times a block
Something fun and charming
No matter which way you walked
Which made exploring such a joy
But as time slithered on
So did the darkening
The blotting out of views
By towering high-rises,
The outward creep
Of a homeless army
From downtown
To camping in area parks,
The demolition of beloved
Neighborhood food cart pods
For more upscale apartments,
The unstoppable crime wave
As junkies brazenly looted
Nearby homes and cars
For anything they could resell
While the police shortage
Ensured nothing at all
Would be done about it,
The combination of all of this
Worked to snuff out the joy
As people brought
The nice things inside
Or they just moved away
As they were priced out
Due to the inevitable gentrification

Showing that Portland was just
A victim of it's own success
As the creatives and unique places
Got crowded out and priced out
To make way for the flocks
Of people, money in hand
Handing it over to developers
And business owners
Craving quantity over quality
Back-turning on what made it
Such a great place to begin with
Not realizing, or caring,
That this continued
Dilution of Portland
Will result in a bland city,
A mere carbon copy
Of everywhere else
Where the good times
Are tethered to the memories
Of the old-timers
Who left long ago

August 24, 2017
Galena, Illinois

I'm glad I was able to experience Portland while it was interesting,
but I am also very happy that we left.

The Incline Is Worth It

There are those who think
The incline is worth it
The knowledge,
The perspective gained from
The increased view
Changes the life
Just enough
To justify the effort it took
To get to that vantage point

August 30, 2017
Galena, Illinois

We have a tiny, miniscule hill in our backyard. While I was out there with the dogs, I thought of the increased views of the higher vantage point and this poem popped into my head.

August

The Cupcake

SEPTEMBER

Only In America

Only in America
Would a rolling coal asshole
Be allowed to make a mockery
Of our planet's life-support system
At the expense of
Health, science, and reason.
Thankfully this societal aberration
Is only happening here
Which gives hope to the land
Where the lamp that once
Was beside and lit the golden door
Has been dropped in the mud,
And run over by a jacked-up truck,
As the door was replaced
By rotting particle-board
Spray-painted gold

September 5, 2017
Galena, Illinois

We've become the embarrassment of the world.

Also, read the Statue Of Liberty poem to see how far we've fallen.

Sooner Sunset

It's 6:59 pm and here I am
Watching the last of the rays
Lighting the day today
As they orange their way
Through the thinning leaves
Of the trees that hide the horizon
I know the Sun doesn't set officially
For another half hour or so
But the fact that this is happening
Before seven o'clock
Is somewhat distressing
Meaning that we're swinging
Fully into autumn
On an express train
That's non-stop charging
As we plow into winter
And here I am, trying
To hang onto every minute
That the waning sunset can give
As the brief summer season
Passes more distantly
With each sooner sunset

September 9, 2017
Galena, Illinois

The rapidly quickening of the passage of time is something I have always had a real problem with. Once in a while I try to plant a marker in my mind ("It's 8:30 pm and the sun is setting," "Wow, only 7:15 pm?" etc). Before I know it, I'll be dark before 5 pm, and then it'll be 2018 and another whole year will be gone. Faster and faster goes each revolution around the Sun. Despite my desires, I know it'll never slow down. I can only work to fill the time as best as I can.

Cats Can Do A Lot

Cats can do a lot
But one thing
They absolutely
Cannot ever do
Is appreciate
The beauty
Of a stunningly
Striking sunset
Because they're
Much too busy
Being well-known
Internet sensations

> September 11, 2017
> Galena, Illinois

That does keep them pretty busy.

A Distant Second

One of
The worst days
To have a birthday
Is today
Because everyone
Will be thinking
About that other thing
First and foremost
And your age
A distant second

September 11, 2017
Galena, Illinois

Whenever I've met someone and they say their birthday is
September 11, the person asking is always like, *"Oh!* Sorry,"
followed by an awkward silence.

Be Quiet For A Few Days

Hurricane Irma showed us
That if you want to
Actually make the
Reality show host–
Turned politician
Be quiet for a few days
That all it takes is a
Bigly natural disaster
The likes of which
Have never been seen

September 11, 2017
Galena, Illinois

The damage and devastation of the hurricane has been enormous.
At the same time, I felt weirdly relaxed and I had a hard time
trying to figure out why…and then it hit me: the news has been
focused on the weather and not on politics for once.

Betrayed By The Shuffle

I was in a random mood
So I hit *shuffle* on my iTunes
And let it serve up whatever
Just something different
From my 30,000 songs
I listened to a few
I skipped a few
I added a few to playlists
I was slain by a few
Whose powerful notes
Were a lead-lined fist
From a previous time
Swinging, connecting
Pounding, pummeling
Assailing me with the feels…
Not wanting to be in that place
I skipped to the next track
And was, once again,
Betrayed by the shuffle
And the hits kept coming
As if someone above
Was in control of my music
Someone who decided I needed
A drive down memory lane
Ripping, shredding, tearing
Down the once-tranquil street
In a monster truck
Hell-bent on doing
As much damage as possible
But, as with all things,
I am the one in charge
So I took control,
Disabled the shuffle,
And went directly
To a happy playlist
And went to a happy place
And had a much better night

The Cupcake

September 15, 2017
Galena, Illinois

Gee whiz, iTunes. What's up with you?

Swan Song Dive

It's just a thing
An exploratory satellite
Launched twenty years ago
To take pictures
Make readings
Launch a probe
And do things
We can't from so far away
It's just a thing
So why did I feel so sad
At listening to the live feed
Of its final minutes
As it was ending
Its swan song dive
Into the atmosphere
To be torn apart,
Crushed, and melted
By the heat and pressure
A tidy end
After it had served its purpose
But why did I feel sad?
Probably because
Things like this
Scientific exploratory things
Are becoming harder to find
In this day and age
Where ignorance
Is valued equally
(and often more)
Than actual knowledge
Here was something
Dedicated to learning
Purposed with discovering
Everything observable
About our planetary neighbors
What they were doing
How they were formed

How they behaved
It gave us a view
To something new
And for that I'm thankful
It's nice to know at one time
We used to want to expand
Our understanding of the universe

Hopefully those days will return
And we will be able to go further
And do more than we ever thought possible

> September 15, 2017
> Galena, Illinois

Goodbye Cassini.

Without End

Essentially
You, me,
Everything
Is energy
According
To science
Proven and
Tested and
A darn fact
We are that
Yes, energy
And energy
Cannot be
Destroyed
So we will
Live onward
Live past this
Current life
And we will
Continue on
Because we
Are energy
You and I
Were once
Star stuff
Everything
Once was
Elements
Within a
Star that
Exploded
Sending out
Its elements
Which ended
Up coalescing
With remnants
From other stars

Which died
And formed
New stars
Planets, and
Eventually us
Recycling
The energy
Over and over
From now
To forever
Without end

September 15, 2017
Galena, Illinois

I ended up listening to "Sans Commentaire" by Autour de Lucie on repeat. It's a unique song and it seemed to drive me as I felt compelled to adhere to the general constraints of the first line's width. Basically, I wrote to the shape first and foremost and whatever was created was unintentional. I think the phrase, "*Sans fin*" (without end) repeating at the end of the song had something to do with the content.

Dechargable Battery

We have a dachshund
A long dog who loves
To be pressed up against
Someone, anyone
On the couch
Or in a chair
And once he's
Lying on his side
And settled into place
By your leg
The dechargable battery
That is his body
Begins its magic
Slowly draining
Your energy
Gently making
You drowsy
Gradually lulling
You into snoozing
Purposefully derailing
Your day and your plans
Because now you're asleep
And that's what he wanted
From the beginning
Because that's just what he does

September 15, 2017
Galena, Illinois

Ugh! Every single time! You'd think after eleven years we would be able to defend ourselves from his nefarious intentions, but no. We can't.

I Used To Do This Thing

I used to this thing
When I'd run across
Someone I used to know
Form a long time ago
Where I would look
At my public self
On different social media
To see how I must look to them
And I wondered what they'd think
Of me, who I am, what I've become
Framed against what they knew of me
From way back then
But now I don't think that way
Because honestly that doesn't do anything
Constructive or helpful in any way
And frankly, I no longer care
What people from the way back
Or people I don't even know think
Because I need my energy positive
And to be focused on where I am
And where I'm going
Not on what someone may
Or may not think

September 15, 2017
Galena, Illinois

Two thoughts unrelated to this poem:
1. It's been two and a half months since we moved and *every single time* I go to type "Galena, Illinois" as the location where I wrote the poem, I start writing "Portland, Oregon" and have to stop, think about it, and correct it.
2. It's actually a little awkward typing the word "Illinois." Try it. It's like your right hand has to do a *Riverdance*-esque jig to get that word out.

A Strangely Underwhelming Process

When I was a kid
Living in the Berkshires
Every autumn I would see
Our country roads clogged
With tourists from out of state
Taking pictures
Taking leaves
And being blown away
By our natural scenery
And I would think to myself:
Don't they have trees?
Don't they have leaves?
Why do they come here
From so far away
Just to look at foliage?

Fast forward to my forties
And living in the Midwest
Where I am now watching
The beginning of autumn
Trees are still mostly green
With leaves that turn slightly
Yellow before dropping
Creating a strangely
Underwhelming process
Making me want to visit
Western Massachusetts
And see some real foliage

September 16, 2017
Galena, Illinois

Apart from very rare slashes of color, the foliage here is terrible so far. I hope it gets better.

We Just Bought A Grill

We just bought a grill
Which I use frequently
I have never felt
More suburban
Or American

September 16, 2017
Galena, Illinois

True story. I got it about a month ago and have used it at least
twice a week since then.

Bucket Of Meat

I needed something quickly
So I made an unaccustomed stop
To my nearby Walmart.
While trying to get my bearings
I passed an endcap cooler
Filled with something called
"Bucket Of Meat."

Dumbfounded, I stopped,
Turned, and got a better look.

Correction:
"Big Bucket Of Meat."

Disgustedly horrified –
By the name of the product,
The lack of further description
Saying what kind of meat
This big bucket contained,
And the sheer amount of it
Spurred me to quickly get
What I had come for
And leave this place
While also putting into question
The culinary choices
Of those in my new community

September 16, 2017
Galena, Illinois

Am I being a food snob? Probably. Should I take into
consideration that many people cannot afford good food? Yes. But
geez, *come on!* We're talking about a big bucket of meat called
"Big Bucket Of Meat."

Potaco

A baked potato
With a V-shaped
Lengthwise wedge
Removed and filled
With ground beef,
Cheese, sour cream,
Lettuce, and sauce
The potaco
Is the best
Of every world

September 18, 2017
Galena, Illinois

I just invented a new food idea! I am so smart! I am so awesome!
Yay, me!

(Google search)

Crap, it's already a thing.
(Sad trumpet sound.)

Party Of Five

The three of us
Entered a restaurant
And waited for
A few minutes
For the hostess to return
When she did
She asked, "How many,"
And a woman who just entered
Stepped in front of us
And replied, "Five,"
Just as I said, "Three"
And her other four
Members of her
Party of five
Stood in front of us
Either oblivious,
Or not caring,
Of our presence
And our position
As being there first
The hostess
Did a double take
And said to the barger,
"I'll be right with you,"
As she said to us,
"Right this way,"
Much to the consternation
And huffy dismay
Of the woman
Who appeared to have felt
That her and her brood
Were snubbed and slighted
At getting a table
At this half-empty restaurant

September 23, 2017
Galena, Illinois

My mom is visiting us for a few days and we stopped in to grab a quick lunch at the Desoto Hotel downtown. While being seated, this happened.

To Ignore The Crisis

For the ones "leading" our country
To ignore the crisis of an island
Ravaged and ruined by a hurricane
And instead focus on their debt
Is like an ambulance arriving
On the scene of a horrific accident
And the EMTs reviewing
The credit scores of the victims
And chiding them at length
For their credit histories
Before lifting a finger to help

September 27, 2017
Galena, Illinois

Every day they out-do themselves on resetting the bar for a new low.

How Deep

On a daily basis
I am constantly,
Continually,
And consistently surprised
At how deep
The stagnant shallow end
Really is

September 27, 2017
Galena, Illinois

That's deep, as in "I am surprised at how many of them there are,"
versus the introspective kind of deep.

Dustbin

One does not let up their grip
Upon the power
They've held so vice-tightly
For centuries
So easily
Which is why
A torrent of teeth gnashing
And melodramatic threats
Flow so loudly
And with such hatred
When they lose
Even the faintest
Hair-width of power
To those they've held down
For untold generations
And here they are
Losing not inches
But miles
As the old guard
Passes on and away
And the young guard
Doesn't share the same
Values or beliefs
Meaning their "way of life"
Is thankfully vanishing
As it's being swept up
And unceremoniously dumped
Into the dustbin of history
Where regressive thinking belongs

September 28, 2017
Galena, Illinois

I had written the bulk of this sometime last year (around the
election when the racists and other horrible people felt embolden to
come out of their hate closet) and just discovered it in my Line

Ideas document. I dusted it off and added to it. Sadly, it's still relevant.

A Purring Yearning

A purring yearning
Melting my resistance
Like snowflakes in lava
As the remembrances
Of events never chanced
Caused action to happen
In a manner unforeseen

September 28, 2017
Galena, Illinois

I was poking around my Line Ideas document and discovered the first three lines of this sitting there, intriguing me. It felt weird and random, so I added a few nonsense lines after it. Short. Silly. Weird. Sometimes it happens.

Tapered Glass

Tapered glass
Impossibly wide at the bottom
Too tiny narrow at the top
At first, we don't realize it's filling
But by the time we bother to notice
We really don't even care
Because there's so much going on
So much to see, so much to do
Much too busy living in the moment
But not appreciating the moment
To see beyond our narrow field of vision
And to consider the top
Or what happens when
The glass is filled
Is a nonexistent thing
Dwelling in the bottom of the glass
Existence seems eternal; an endless buffet of life
It fills a little more each day, and we take it
A little more for granted than the day before
Because that's just how it is, that's how things are
Then societal norms take root and envelop
Dictating how things should be "just so"
But, as time passes, as it tends to do
You find yourself surprised at how
Quickly the glass is filling
But no matter what you do
You can't stop the flow
As each point you place
To mark off the time
Gets passed more
Quickly than it had
The last time
Again and
Again it
Slips by
Faster
Until

Full
The tapered glass fills completely and overspills its boundaries
rendering it useless

September 28, 2017
Galena, Illinois

This was another fragment of an idea sitting in Line Ideas that I
expanded upon.

That Decade Shouldn't Count

Each block of time
Seems so unique
And like it's own thing
So different from the rest
The sixties
The seventies
The eighties
The nineties
The two-thousands?
That decade shouldn't count
And neither should this one
The one we're currently in
Because nothing about it
Is particularly distinctive,
Fun, interesting, or positive
In a way which will make us,
Decades from now,
Look back fondly
As the time we're in

> September 28, 2017
> Galena, Illinois

I think we're in the first time period that will be skipped, or
glossed over, by nostalgia.

All The Above

Doing things we look forward to
Doing things we don't want to do
Sleeping in
Working hard
Fun things
Obligatory things
All the above
Sometimes that's just what a day is about

September 28, 2017
Galena, Illinois

OCTOBER

The Empire Of The Night

The light shifts from full-lit day
Into the swinging tint of hue-blue night
The leafless squirrel highways,
Formally bark-brown and khaki,
Become silhouetted blood vessels
Connecting the graying green down
To the navying blue of the dome above.

This in-between hour is dangerous for both
As the two sides, weakened, can be out
At the same time, although none prefer it
The late-day shift awakens, emboldens,
And brings The Empire Of The Night
Fully onto the scene of everything
As the rotation gives rise to their strength
When the color is drained and replaced
With nothing but the noticeable lack of it.

Yes, lights go on but their radius is small
And cannot hope to safeguard or compete
With what is coming, so they enter, lock,
And hide behind their protective doors
Draw their blinds, and light up their homes
And try to push, block, and will it all away
As if simply pretending it's not out there
And assuage the fears of what the mind knows
And the heart refuses to face.

In the dark, the once-gentle wind has been changed,
Twisted, corrupted, degraded into something sinister
Not evil in its own right, but the forbearer of such.
It seeks, searches, reaches, touches, and finds those out
With a playful tousle through the hair, as if comforting
The soon-to-be departed in a way greatly perverting
The touch of the same interplay during the daytime.
When it finds a being of the day, it sends a howl aloud
Signaling to the darkened denizens of potential prey

October

To feel the chilling wind is to feel the snap of the whip
Against the unprotected skin, tightening, puckering it
Like the sickly yellow fleshy rind of long-dead poultry
While it makes the body underneath crawl with paranoia
Causing the mind to act hastily and irrationally
Sending it careening into any one of a thousand dangers.

For those lingering too long in the falling dusk
Hope is hard to find and harder to hold and keep close as
Those equipped with foreknowledge enough to bring a light
Will find the spot of illumination to be exceptionally small,
Wavering with trepidation, and becoming increasingly dim;
Subdued and fearly weakened by the closing, hungry night.
Only the foolhardy dare to risk their summation of life,
On what surmounts to nothing more than a route to a quick end.
It is unknown what is to be gained by attempting the impossible
And tempting fate, nevertheless they continue to do so in droves
Leaving behind nothing but tattered shreds, a sign of a struggle,
And families grieving while placing headstones over empty graves.

In this sinister hour, familiar objects take on new looks
And are reinterpreted by the eyes in loomingly sinister new ways.
One night, the row of trees in a backyard may seem like
The long, unkempt, stiffly stubble of an earth giant in repose
Aware of the intruder who dares to trod upon his cheek
Nights later, those same trees take on a whole new look
The reaching, twisting appendages of a baleful unknown
Which can only be described as squid-like as they sway,
Creak, groan, and reach for the trespasser on its land.
Some say the trees act as spyful sentinels keeping watch,
Keeping track, while doing their best to obscure and scare,
Frighten and waylay, and trip up and ensnare the unprepared.

The creeping fog approaches, devouring sanity and light
Reducing visibility, diminishing hope, engulfing rationality
Further seeking to disorientate and confuse the hapless
Into making a wrong turn, steering them away from safety
And into one of the thousands of other deadly deceptions
Waiting for the hapless stragglers in the rising darkness

Where the wolves, never ever seen, provide the soundtrack
The close-by, chilling background sound adding to the
Fearsome feeling causing the unfortunates to run, reeling
From the haunting reverberations and the enclosing mist.

The quick scurrying movements punctuating the darkness
Serve to jolt and keep the unfortunate on perpetual edge
As the small creatures, too fast to see, swarm just out of sight
However, it's the loud and direct steps of the larger beasts,
The things who fear nothing, that one must worry about
Once they are first heard, the unlucky do not stand a chance
While they may seem solitary, the larger beasts work in tandem
With the rest of the shadowy symphony culminating in a extended
Work of art comprised of the unlimited means and methods
To create fear, dread, and utter despondent hopelessness
Before finally finishing off their prey in a protracted way
As this malevolent performance continues and replays
From the sinking of the sun until the following morning
When the rays of light rise, revealing the terrifying extent
To which the Empire Of The Night ruled the darkness.

October 1, 2017
Galena, Illinois

I've worked on this one here and there for the past five years. I got
the idea for it one night when I lived in Vermont and was walking
the dogs in the dusky darkness in late autumn. The combination of
the faint light, the leafless trees, and the encroaching shadows
made everything seem super creepy. This definitely is not the kind
of thing I normally write, but I was hoping to capture that feeling
with this poem.

Perfectly Patriotic

Driving just before sunset
And something caught my eye
A flag, high atop its pole –
Caught, shining, in the ideal light
Rippling in that flawless manner
Like consistent little waves
Creating a head-turning scene
That was perfectly patriotic in every way
Something you would normally see
Only in computer animations
On wrestling shows, truck commercials,
Or overly nationalistic news programs
Never in real life and never like this
An event in Middle America
Noticed by no one but me
Despite the flag sitting right there
In a busy Walmart parking lot
Where half the vehicles were stickered
With faded Chinese-made variations
Depicting the taken-for-granted object
On glorious display for all to see

October 1, 2017
Galena, Illinois

I mean, the flag could not have looked more perfect in that
moment. The last rays of the setting sun warmly illuminating the
highly-perched flag, rippling with the ideal breeze creating small
sine-wave-like ripples consistently giving even rolling in the fabric
that was not too strong and not too weak. It was stunningly ideal to
the point of making me realize that in life you hardly ever see such
a perfectly-staged scene naturally occur.

As an Eagle Scout, I know how the flag should be displayed and it
seems like more often than not, it's not being displayed correctly;
as if the patriotism of the displayer takes precedence over the

proper, respectful way it should be presented. This though, was like nature conspired to create something impressive in that minute.

I listened to "Play Money" by The New Pornographers on repeat while writing this.

Without Ceremony

This time of the year
The Sun sets
Too easily
Too quickly
As it sinks
Below the treetops
Without ceremony
Or spectacle
Like it used to
In the summer months
Oh, here and there
It might swath the clouds
With a pastel paintbrush
But even that is over
Quicker than you can
Pull your phone out
To capture the moment
Almost as if the Sun
Has given up on us
Like we already did

October 2, 2017
Galena, Illinois

It's time for my annual bunch of "The Sun sets too damn early"-poems.

Spin The Shooter

Shrouded in the uncertain immediacy
Instantly following the national tragedy
All parties assemble to throw their words
Out there, into the unsuspecting world,
So they can be the ones to spin the shooter
To tell the narrative their side needs
To sell the story their side wants
In a manner consistent with their objectives
It doesn't matter if it's later proven false
The primary goal is to be out there first
Because that will be what is picked up
And re-broadcast over and over again
To sway the public mindset on this event
Retractions and corrections will be released
But no one pays attention to those footnotes
Because the belief has already been firmed up
Like a teenager's scrawl in wet concrete
The impression will last well longer
In our public consciousness
Than the event itself

October 2, 2017
Galena, Illinois

Sickening.

When You Knew

It's almost as if
This moment deserves
Special recognition
For being a snippet of life
That goes above and beyond
The normal moments we endure
Which make up the bulk of existence
Because this is the instant
When it hit you
Hard
In the gut
When you *knew*
Eleven billionty percent
And everything clicked into place
In a manner so perfect
That you cannot help but believe
In predestination
Because this was,
Without any doubt,
A coincidence's coincidence
One of those moments in our lives
You can count on one hand
Where the spark in your heart
Confirmed with absolutely certainty
That this was meant to be

October 2, 2017
Galena, Illinois

I'm not a fast writer of poetry. Most of my poems are half a page to a page and they take, on average, 20 to 30 minutes to write. I had no idea what I was going to write when I started this one and it was complete within five minutes while listening to the Sufjan Stevens song, "Chicago." I guess writing from the heart is made easier with a song like this, which is liquid beauty in your ears.

Michael Newton would call this moment in life, I described with this poem, as a "Recognition signal."

Autumn Olympics

I had a dream last night
Somewhat of the absurd kind
Where I speculated
On something that doesn't exist
On what the Autumn Olympics
Would look like
Firstly, it would probably always
Be set in autumnal New England
And the roster of sporting events
Would include things like

Raking –
How quickly you could sweep up
An acre of fallen foliage
Spread out over a hilly lawn

Corn maze slalom –
Successfully navigating
A huge corn maze for the gold
Without getting lost or tripped up

Biathlon Carving –
Hit the pumpkin carving station first
Before racing across town to the in-laws
To debone the Thanksgiving turkey

Haunted hayride –
Get through the entire course
Filled with spooky delights
Without your blood pressure spiking

Country fair –
Make your way through the day
Without once losing your cool
With anyone; family or stranger

Bake off –

The Cupcake

Battle against several moms
To create the pie of the season
For a party of influential judges

Photography –
Shoot the perfect autumnal scene
And post it to get more Instagram likes
Than your competitors in the time limit

Artisan cocktails –
Impress the judges with the best
Signature cocktail to end the evening
Using the best blend of spices

All-in-all
This version of the Olympics
Sounds much more appealing
Than anything that has been
Attempted previously
And I think it merits
More study and implementation

October 2, 2017
Galena, Illinois

All I remember is waking up in the middle of the night and
entering "Autumn Olympics" into the Notes app on my phone
while I was still mostly asleep.

Filter

Now, more than ever
We need to filter
We need to weed out
All the negativity
All the shit we're hit with
Constantly
Consistently
Every day
And replace it
With positivity
Something, anything,
Constructive, nice,
And good-feeling
Because we need to be
Built up and empowered
Not worn down
And weighed down
With hopelessness and fear
Delete news feeds
From your social media
Avoid comment sections
And do whatever feels
Good and right for you
And you will realign yourself
And be a freer and better
Version of yourself
Almost immediately

October 3, 2017
Galena, Illinois

I'm not saying bury your head in the sand, but a conscious
avoidance of heavy, overtly negative stories and situations will do
you a world of good.

A Comet Knows The Way

A comet knows the way
The tail points away
From gravity's light
Full of blazing action
In its cosmic loop-de-loop
Forever orbiting the Sun

> October 3, 2017
> Galena, Illinois

Most of this was in Line Ideas. I thought it was fun and brief so I cleaned it up. Ta-da.

I Will Gladly Trade

I will gladly trade the background sounds
The din of taxis, honking, shouting,
And the stifled, short deadened breath
For gentle chirping, wind though the leaves,
And the fullness of fresh, natured air

October 3, 2017
Galena, Illinois

Had I Been A Zygote

Groceries in hand
Walking back to my car
In the Piggly Wiggly parking lot
When I saw a white Buick
Engine on, old woman at the wheel
Putting the car into reverse
Without first looking
To see what, or who,
She was about to run over.
I sidestepped and slapped her trunk
As her *All Life Is Precious*
Bumper sticker brushed my leg
Her incredulous look told me
She was equally surprised
By my being behind her
And also indignant of my gall
To dare touch her automobile.
Once I was clear or her radius
She sped out of there
Narrowly missing a pedestrian
And running a stop sign.
I am tempted to believe
That had I been a zygote
She would have practiced
An abundance of caution
But chances are pretty good
She would have squished me
Without notice or thought

October 5, 2017
Galena, Illinois

What's even more annoying than almost being run over is that this
grocery store does not have cart corrals in the parking lot so you
have to return the carts inside the store when you're done. Really?

Do we live in some dark version of the past before futuristic conveniences like cart corrals were invented? Geez.

Surround Yourself

Surround yourself
With good feeling
And you will experience
A really great day

October 5, 2017
Galena, Illinois

A little too short (like fortune cookie short), but it's something
that's been on my mind. I'm a pretty positive person, in general,
but I am working to make a conscious effort to increase my
positive vibration.

Heavy In My Mouth

The words
Are heavy
In my mouth
And constantly
Threatening
To fall out

October 7, 2017
Galena, Illinois

While at the Galena Country Fair today, Kari said something roughly along these lines.

Maybe It Serves As A Warning

While at the town's
Annual fall fair
I saw a woman walk by
With the following words
Tattooed on her upper arm:
Smiling now
Crying later
And it made me wonder
How much must someone
Love, wholly identify with,
And so fully embrace
Their depressive sadness
To get those words
Forever indelibly inked into
A prominent part of their flesh
Maybe it serves as a warning
To others that this person
Comes with a freight train
Of emotional baggage

                    October 7, 2017
                    Galena, Illinois

Warning! Warning! Warning!

Braved The Drizzle

Yesterday
It was cloudy
And occasionally
A little rainy
But mostly
It was drizzly
So we took advantage
Of the weather,
Braved the drizzle,
And went outside
And enjoyed
The town's annual
Country fair
And were rewarded
With short lines,
Room to move,
And the time
To fully appreciate
Everything there.

Today
It is sunny
And warm
And our town
Is overwhelmed
With wall-to-wall
People everywhere
And I can only imagine
That trying to get through
Those mobbing crowds
Must be a maddening
Terrible undertaking
The mere thought
Of which makes
Me thankful
We went yesterday.

October 8, 2017
Galena, Illinois

We live a half mile from Grant Park where the Galena Country Fair is being held and our entire street is lined with parked cars. Nuts. I'm so glad we went yesterday.

Acceptance Is A Small Silent Room

Acceptance is a small silent room
More restrictive than hoped
Boxed in by constraining beliefs
Acknowledgment of limitations
Where freedom is acquiesced
In exchange for quietness
And to ensure that nothing
Will change beyond the confines
Of what was agreed upon

October 9, 2017
Galena, Illinois

Charge The Line

It's only when I'm
Deep in my flutters
Do I express my druthers
Motivate the men
Hop on my horse
And charge the line
Of the blank page
The clackening
Of the fingers
Filling the space
Like the hoofbeats
Rhythmically beating
Bearing down
On my targeted goal
Faster and faster
Until it is complete
And I have won

> October 9, 2017
> Galena, Illinois

This was in Line Ideas for probably five or six years.

Evolve Into The Better Version

A long time gone
Since the trial run
Went from serious
To officially official
Not as long has passed
Since it all imploded
The way it was destined
To leave me in the right place
To pick up and move on
Allowing me the introspection
To analyze, make corrections
And evolve into the better version
That I have since become

October 10, 2017
Galena, Illinois

My first (starter) wife and I got married 19 years ago today. We separated four years later. I am thankful for that experience because it allowed me to evolve into a much better version of myself and find the right person; both of which would not have happened had I not been released from that union. The perspective of freedom is wonderful and eye-opening.

Running Empty

In a Walmart parking lot,
Where too many recent
Poems seem to start,
And I heard the guttural
Chugga-chugga-chugga
Of an oversized truck
Idling noisily nearby
Which got me wondering
Why do so many people
Seem to hang out here
In a Walmart parking lot?
But as I looked, I noticed
The truck was empty
Completely devoid
Of human occupants
Meaning the driver
Drove his pickup here,
Got out, went inside,
And is in there shopping
While his truck is out here
Running empty
For no other reason
Than the act of turning it off
And turning it back on
Were just too taxing
So here it is
Wasting gas,
I assume unlocked,
Completely ready
And available
To be had for a steal

October 12, 2017
Galena, Illinois

Maybe it's just the mindset of someone who is used to living in a small town where everyone knows everyone else, but leaving your vehicle running in the parking lot while you're inside just seems insane to me. I see it all the time at the Casey's gas station/convenience store as well. I don't think I could ever be that lazy, or trusting.

Where The Signal Is Reliable

A tiny village
So far away form everything
Twenty minutes to the next town
Forty to the closest small city
(With a decent supermarket)
The kind of place where
The only cell reception
Can be found across the street
In the shared parking lot
For the library
(Only open ten hours a week),
Town hall
(And *museum*),
And the old cemetery
Up behind on the hill.
So at all hours of the night
Cars will pull over there
Where the signal is reliable
And they talk
(Usually with the windows down)
With their far-away family,
Their non-spousal lovers,
And other people they need to call
With the privacy
That the land-line
Cannot provide
So I sit on my front porch,
Completely secretly,
And listen to their lives

October 12, 2017
Galena, Illinois

I wrote the first smattering idea of this back around 2012 when we
lived in Benson, Vermont.

The Relish Backdrop

While making a sandwich
I stare out the kitchen window
At the vermilion sunset
Breaking brightly through
The hole in the clouds
And watch with interest
As the light illuminates
The leaves like
An autumnal rock show
Twisting and dancing
Dripping the raindrops
In the brisk October wind
Reminding me about today
Where I have been diligently
Trying to ignore the calendar
Saying it is currently
Friday the thirteenth
A number which has nothing,
Nothing at all, to do with
The melancholy mustard
I'm slathering
On the relish backdrop
Of this sandwich
I have no intention of eating

October 13, 2017
Galena, Illinois

Tonight I am going to my first Dubuque Area Writers Guild
meeting. On their Facebook page they had a challenge to write a
poem, prose, or essay using any one (or all) of the following
words:

mustard
brisk
leaves

relish
sunset
thirteen
raindrop
vermilion
melancholy

I managed to squeeze all of them in there.

Follow-up: No one from the Dubuque Area Writers Guild showed up to their own meeting, so my poem went unread.

Motivation

Motivation
To get things done
Is often in short supply
As the stone at rest
Is apt to stay that way
In its comfortable rut
Covered in a cozy covering
Of moss that's warming
Making it that much harder
To get moving
To get rolling
In the direction
It needs to go

> October 16, 2017
> Galena, Illinois

Me!

Prideful Ignorance

I'm not sure when it started
Or became fashionable
But the deep belief
In prideful ignorance
Where being
Overtly oblivious,
Distrusting knowledge,
Openly hating success,
Antagonizing correctness,
Maintaining deeply-rooted biases,
Preserving homogeny,
And generally living no deeper
Than skimming the surface
Is celebrated to such an extent
Where this witlessness
Is held in the same regard
As the summation of humanity's
Shared scientific achievements
And our society's social mores
Are a thing of cultural contempt
And the mere act of critical thinking
Is now critically endangered
By a population hell-bent on "stigginit"

October 16, 2017
Galena, Illinois

The Volcano Within

Feeling the fury building
Shaking with energy
Struggling to contain
The volcano within
Smoking
Burning
Rising
Approaching
The line of uncontainability
When crossed
Will explode beyond the box
Like a supernova
Destroying everything
We've ever known
And erasing existence
With indelible permanence

October 16, 2017
Galena, Illinois

Yikes-a-rooni! I wanted to listen to my "Anger – Heavy" iTunes
playlist and see what it would inspire me to write.

Such A Beautiful Day That I Don't Want To Share

It's such a beautiful day
That I don't want to share it
With you
Or anyone else
(no offense)
I want this, the endless sea
Of richly-hued blue sky
I want this, the effortless being
Surrounded by the ideal temperature
I want this, the foliage alight
Piquing the peek as they peak
I want this, the autumnal bouquet
Better than any jar candle
I want this, the cool breeze
Describing of what's to come
I want this, the day ahead of me
Completely free to enjoy just like this
Taking it all in
And appreciating the beauty
Filling my view today

October 17, 2017
Galena, Illinois

Wow. It was a perfect day outside today

When The Tree's Pants Drop

Leaves are nature's clothing
Effortlessly concealing
Everything that's over there
The far stuff a street away
To the back of the house stuff
Like twiggy branches
And squirrelly houses
That we're surprised to see
When the tree's pants drop
Shockingly revealing
Everything that's been there
Unseen, the entire time

October 23, 2017
Galena, Illinois

I'm always so surprised by what I can actually see once the leaves are on the ground.

Working On Redemption

The bar is the alter
The stools are the pews
Of the congregation
Facing the minister
Who dispenses wisdom
With each individual's
Preferred variation
Of heavenly salvation
With the most faithfully
Devoted praying here
Each and every day
Working on redemption

October 23, 2017
Galena, Illinois

Devotion takes many forms.

Swept Into Action

Swept into action
By an unlikely source
When I was ready
To shut it all down
And from nowhere
Came the motivation
Lifting me to my feet
Shoving me along –
Stumbly slow at first
Catching the rhythm
Getting in the groove
And driving me onward
To a future uncertain
With the only given
Is that now I'm moving

October 23, 2017
Galena, Illinois

I was just about to close Microsoft Word and go play Team Fortress 2 when "Disintegration" by The Cure started playing on my iTunes. The driving beat of the song, coupled with the fact that it's been three and a half years since I've last heard this song, gave me the motivation to continue writing. Sometimes when you're ready to be done, the Universe steps in with other plans for you.

The Idyllic Scene

The warming comfort
Of a wood stove's heat
On a cold winter's night
The sweet relaxation
Of a wine's warmth
Radiating through me
The deep reassurance
Of a soulmate's shoulder
Pressing against my own
The dancing magical light
Of the surrounding candles
Completing the idyllic scene

October 23, 2017
Galena, Illinois

The song, "The First Taste" by Fiona Apple came on and it made me feel this.

The Slow Reveal

Two months in the making
The slow reveal is taking shape
As our scenery is thinning out
Showing everything
Nature saw fit to hide
During the summering months

October 29, 2017
Galena, Illinois

Writing Is A Solitary Endeavor

When I lived in Portland
I was surrounded by
Books, writers,
Writing groups,
Writing conferences,
Literary journals,
The largest independent bookstore,
The most active public library system,
And more great writing resources
Than I could shake a keyboard at
And, strangely, I never once
Took advantage of any of it.

I moved 2,000 miles away
To a rural Midwest town
Where, upon landing,
I actively sought out
Any and all literary resources
Determined to join a community
Of like-minded creatives.
I went to the Writers Guild
Across the river in Dubuque
To the meeting place and time
Posted on their Facebook group
Only to find myself alone
Because no one showed up
Save for me and two others
Who had never been
And also wanted to join
So we had our own meeting
Despite not knowing
What we were doing.

In the meantime
I discovered there's a group
Of writers in my own town
With no website or online presence

They proved tricky to track down
But I sent emails to two members
Asking how to join their organization.
Days later I received my replies:
One, who runs the local arts center,
Decried how the town library
"Terminated" their program
Left them without a place to meet,
And told me to contact the librarian
And convince her to reinstate their group.
The other replied and told me
That she's not sure if they're
Letting new people join them,
That they'll discuss it
At their next meeting
In November.

Two weeks had passed
And it was time for the
Dubuque group's meeting
So I drove out there
Hoping that someone
Would actually attend
And once again
I was alone.
The owner of the bar/café said
They've been "flakey" lately
And haven't seen them much.

So, I'm faced with one group
Where the members
Don't care enough to show up
And another giving
Conflicting information
But in the end
Seem to treat their group
Like a secret society
Wary of outsiders.

The Cupcake

Despite my repeated efforts
To join a group of writers
And be with others like me
I'm finding myself in the same place
Proving yet again
What I already knew to be true:
Writing is a solitary endeavor
And all I really need is me.

October 29, 2017
Galena, Illinois

I've really been trying to get involved in the local literary
community, which apparently does not give any flying flips about
new members who are looking to participate. No biggie. I am quite
content on doing my own thing.

I Cannot Be Less

I cannot be less
Than what I am
Which is expanding
And getting greater
Every single day

> October 29, 2017
> Galena, Illinois

I seem to like following long poems with wee little ones.

NOVEMBER

The Emotional Toll

The emotional toll
Effectively totals
The summation
Of energies spent
Worrying, stressing,
Wracking the heart,
The mind, and the soul
Working in concert
Day after day after day
Draining the life
Reducing the will
To continue; to live

November 5, 2017
Galena, Illinois

My life is normally pretty darn spiffy, but once in a while, when I'm feeling particularly sad for a few hours, it feels like my energy has been drained completely. I can't imagine how people who are depressed for extended periods of time, can continue to function at all.

Used Sparingly, To Taste

Things are so much different now
Everything has been sharpened to the extreme
There's no way to recapture and relive
The simplicity and the innocence
We experienced in our youth
It was exchanged for two things:
Convenience and knowledge
The first we have come to expect at all costs
The second is strangely being used sparingly,
To taste, like a flavor additive or a seasoning
Instead of being served as the main course
As was intended by those before us
The ones who worked hard and passed it down
The ones who wanted us to live better lives
And instead of feasting and celebrating
The enhanced utopian science fiction
Reality we should be currently living in
We huddle here, filling up on reality shows,
Loudly flaunting our ignorance
And proudly voting against our own interests
As everything that had been built
Over the past two centuries
As our collective identity
Is rotting, collapsing,
Before our very eyes
Into the country-wide debris heap
Of our nation's diminished dreams

November 5, 2017
Galena, Illinois

It's interesting to witness the end of an empire from the inside.
This is the kind of thing you just read about in history books.
Thirty years ago the US and the Soviet Union were the two main
world superpowers. Our standing on the world stage has eroded to
the point where we are no longer held up as the idea to strive for.

Germany and China seem to have taken on the leadership roles among the world's governments. Am I sad about this? No. It's just interesting to see happen and be cognizant of it.

A Silly Thought

A silly thought
That crossed my mind
Late last night
While walking my dogs
What would you call
A dog breed
Where you mixed
A dachshund
With a pug?
Would it be
A "poxie" or a "dug"?
Both are equally silly

November 5, 2017
Galena, Illinois

I warned you in the title that it was a silly thought.

Mental Confetti

I felt a hint of a memory
Like a bit of mental confetti
For a long-forgotten parade
Which passed by years ago
And got caught on the wind
Eventually landing somewhere
Hidden and waiting
For the right breezy moment
To send it airborne again
Bringing the overlooked thought
Back to the forefront
Of my present mind

November 7, 2017
Galena, Illinois

I saw a leaf blowing while walking the dogs yesterday and for some reason thought, "Huh. That leaf looks like a piece of confetti. What if confetti were like memories of some long-ago ticker-tape parade?" Then I had to clean up after my dogs, so I forgot about it until today.

Neverdones

My list of neverdones
For when I lived in Portland
Is a lot longer
Than I'm confortable with
All of the things
I meant to do
But just never
Got around to
Like going to the Rose Parade,
Or the Pride Parade for that matter,
Visiting the Tillamook Cheese Factory
Way out there on the coast,
Disco night tubing at that ski place
On the side of Mount Hood,
Going to Sauvie Island,
Or The Grotto at Christmas time,
Or the holiday Zoo Lights,
Or the Christmas light boat parade
Sailing up the Willamette River,
Going to ComicCon at the convention center,
Attending the Wordstock literary conference,
Finding the very first Geocache location
Twenty miles outside of the city,
Going to *Rocky Horror* at the Clinton,
Seeing a show at Mississippi Studios,
Checking out the Night Market,
Spending a night hopping from
Dive bars to fancy bars on Hawthorne,
Going to the Cornelius Pass Roadhouse,
Or attending a Timbers or Thorns game,
Seeing a show at the Schnitzer Center,
Experiencing Crater Lake,
Or the Painted Hills,
Or that planned forest
Out near Pendleton,
And, Pendleton as well,
Or sailing on a boat

The Cupcake

On the Columbia River,
Or under the St. John's Bridge,

Then there's the wish-I'd-dones
Like spend more time at Edgefield,
And finishing my McMenamins passport,
And eat at Wild Abandon more often,
And go to the Mount Tabor
Adult Soap Box Derby more than once,
And see Cannon Beach and Astoria
More than just that one time,
Same with The Rose Test Garden,
And visiting the city of Bend,
And honestly,
Just wishing we had spent more time
With our friends who are now
Two thousand miles
And two time zones away

> November 7, 2017
> Galena, Illinois

I'm sure there's a LOT more I could have added here but it's what I could come up with in a few minutes. After we moved away from Huntsville, Alabama, we had a lot of regrets of things we didn't see or do while we were in the region (like going to Rock City, or New Orleans, or visiting Chattanooga more than that one time, etc). When we moved to Portland, we vowed to make the most of the experience. While we did do and see a lot of great things there, we obviously missed quite a bit. Now that we're in a whole new region of the country, we have a whole new list of cool things to see and experience in the Midwest. Will we see and do it all? Probably not, but this is a good reminder to get out more and experience what this area has to offer.

Full Moon Skylight

Full moon skylight
Shining down on me
In my middle of the night
Trip to the bathroom
Projecting a silhouette of me
On the wall at a weird angle
With my beadheady tufts
Being the prominent feature
Of my shadowy self

> November 7, 2017
> Galena, Illinois

I Fear For The Future

I fear for the future
When we look back to now
Think of how naïve we were
And how things
Were so much simpler
Back then
Before everything
Became complicated

> November 11, 2017
> Galena, Illinois

It seems that any time we've looked back to a point a decade or three in the past, we've thought, "Oh man, things were just so much simpler then," even though, at the time, life felt cutting edge and complicated. I can't imagine the future when things on this planet become even more extreme to the point where this time, right now, feels "simple."

Book World

There might be a lesson
That can be learned
From witnessing
A bookstore chain
Called "Book World"
Unable to adapt
To the changing climate
Of modern day retail
And is liquidated
Before going under
Celebrated only by
Local paper headlines
Gleefully punning:
"Final chapter for book seller"

> November 11, 2017
> Galena, Illinois

A few weeks ago I noticed the location in my town had a nicely placed "Local Authors" section so I told the woman behind the counter that I was a local author and asked what I had to do to get my books on that shelf.

She scoffed and asked, "How local are you? We don't consider Chicago to be local." She said something else I can't remember now about how they only put real authors on the shelves.

Uh, ok. I told her I lived right in town, about half a mile away. I said I'm the author of nine books but I'm only interested in getting my most recent book (*2492: Attack Of The Ancient Cyborg*) on the shelf.

She shook her head. "There's a very complicated form that needs to be filled out. Book world is a *very* large company. We have 45 locations around the Midwest."

At this point I was thinking, *This woman seems very resistant to helping me.* I said, "If that's all it takes, I don't think I'd have any problems filling out a form."

She retorted, "I'm not the manager. I *used* to be the manager but I'm not anymore. You'll have to talk to the manager and she'll be in on Monday after 3pm. She's the only one who can approve new books but she's only been here for two weeks. She's not very quick and she doesn't know what's going on so she won't know how to do it. It's very complicated and I'll have to show her."

I thought, *Why the hell is she telling me this?* "Ok, I'll be back on Monday."

On Monday I returned at 3pm to find a very friendly woman standing behind the counter with the grumpy old woman. I told her that I was looking to get my book in the Local Authors shelf.

"No problem." She pulled out a piece of paper, "Just fill out this simple form."

While I was filling out the form (name, address, phone, book title, number of copies…and that's it), someone came to the counter to buy a book. The cranky woman said to her, "Do you know how to ring someone up?" and then to the customer, "She's only been here for two weeks."

The new manager said, "Oh yes, and I've been here over month now." She scanned the book and completed the transaction effortlessly. She then took my completed form, gave me a receipt and put my books on the shelf.

Yesterday, when I read the news that the whole bookstore chain was closing, I went down there and picked up my books. The new manager was there, and despite facing losing her new job with the closure, she was still super friendly and personable. I feel bad for her, but with that attitude, she won't have a problem finding something better.

Writing Instead Of Choring

Late Saturday morning
And I'm at my desk
Writing instead of choring
While trying not to feel bad about it
As these poems will be lasting
Whereas after the chores are done
I'll need to do them again
In a short amount of time
And nothing will change
If I put them off for a few hours
Except that I'll feel a lot better
Having written these thoughts

November 11, 2017
Galena, Illinois

Ok, I'm off to put up our outdoor Christmas lights. It's early, I know, but I want have them ready before Kari returns from her work trip to California. Also, we've never once put up outdoor lights anywhere we've lived, so I'm kind of excited about this.

1,000

From the awkward start
Of *Anything But Dreams*
Up through every collection
I've published over the years
And including this very poem
I've written a grand total of
1,000
1,000 separate thoughts
Committed to keyboard
1,000 little stories
Each one a part of me
1,000 observations
Shared with you
Some great,
Some silly,
Some profound,
Some just dumb
But every one of them
Giving you a glimpse
Of something old
Seen in a different way
Or something new
Never considered
Either way
I'm very happy
To have reached
This milestone
With you along
For the ride

> November 11, 2017
> Galena, Illinois

At my current rate of writing, I'll probably hit 2,000 poems in
2026 or 2027*.

Note: As a handy frame of reference, Emily Dickinson wrote 1797 poems in her lifetime. I am in no way comparing myself to her, I'm just noting that she wrote an ass-ton of poems.

*Ugh! Those years seem equally futuristic and really far away. I do not even want to think of how old I'll be then**.

**Too late.)=

I Saw Your Contrail

I knew the approximate time
I knew the path you'd take
I verified the assumption online
And as I was ready to leave
I looked upward to the north
I saw your contrail
A draftsman-perfect line
Tracing west to east
Pointing the way
To where you'd be

November 16, 2017
Galena, Illinois

Kari was returning from a work trip today, so I was following her flight on FlightAware. When I left the house to start driving to the airport to pick her up, I looked up and saw the contrail her plane made.

Wide Load

At the light I turned the corner
Onto the Route 20 bridge
Crossing the little river
Cutting through our town
And didn't get far before
A beat up Crown Victoria
In the oncoming lane
With a *WIDE LOAD* banner
Duct taped across the hood
And several stickers stuck
To the windshield saying,
JESUS and *LIVE, LAUGH, LOVE*
Veered strongly and purposely
Across the double yellow
Aiming at the car in front of me,
Which stopped quickly
To avoid being rammed,
By the *WIDE LOAD* driver
Who rolled his window down
And screamed at the car in my lane
While pointing angrily to the truck
Hundreds of feet behind him
Lumbering our way slowly
Carrying a portion of a house
Meanwhile behind me
The cars turning onto the bridge
Came to a stop mid-intersection
Gridlocking traffic every which way
When the light changed
Effectively blocking the path
The *WIDE LOAD* needed to go
So we all sat there waiting
For the angry guy to do something
When he clearly wasn't capable
Of handling this vehicular situation
He was responsible for creating
Which ended up being solved

By the other intersected drivers
Who safely navigated on by
Ignoring the frantic yelling
And frenzied arm waiving
Of the methy-looking man
Charged with navigating
And clearing the way
For the *WIDE LOAD* truck
Which people avoided
Just fine by themselves

November 18, 2017
Galena, Illinois

A weird scene. Had I been in the car ahead of me and that guy was screaming at me, I would have pointed at his windshield and said, "It looks like someone needs to 'live, laugh, love," before ignoring him and continue driving. Seriously, the truck he was supposed to be in front of was over 300 feet behind him and there were several other vehicles between him and the truck.

The Dusty Remnants

In an aisle
At the local Walmart
Sat a palate
Of Chex-brand cereals
On sale
But while the display
Was hardly touched
The two boxes
Of *FREE* party mix
Seasoning packets
Had been viciously
Stripped bare
To the point
Where all they contained
Were the dusty remnants
Of a torn packet
Someone shredded
In their haste
To get
Something, *anything*,
For free

November 18, 2017
Galena, Illinois

I'm staring to feel weird that too many of my poems lately are
starting with "At the local Walmart," but then again, it never fails
to be a continued source of material to write about.

Wallet Your Ripple

"Wallet your Ripple"
Is a phrase that sounds
Completely crazy
And out-there bonkers
Like a made-up
String of words
Entirely unrelated
Like a Captcha created
By a drunk computer
Yet it's something
I just said in an email
Where I was being
Honest and helpful
Instructing a friend
On how to do a thing

>   November 22, 2017
>   Galena, Illinois

Kind of like going back thirty years and saying to someone, "Let me take a picture of that with my phone."

Their Peephole Worldview

Bored waiting in a hair salon
For a haircut that would never come
Staring out the window
At the trucks passing by
On Route 20
In this rural town
Hours away from
The nearest big city
I overheard two women talking
About the Weinsteining in Hollywood
Lensed through their peephole worldview
With one commenting,
"You've got to wonder
 Why they waited so long,"
And adding,
"If it's just one person
 You can't trust them,
 When more say it too,
 Well, they're probably
 Telling the truth."
And the other saying,
"Some women you can't believe
 But some you can, you know."
I tuned them out,
Favoring the traffic
Of the trucks rumbling by
On their way west
Across the Mississippi
Or going the other way
Toward Chicago
And I hoped
That these two women
Or anyone they knew
Or loved
Were ever in that kind of a situation
Where people would judge them
On whether or not

They could be believed
Based on how many others
Came forward with
Similar stories
Or were left alone
With their ignored claim
Facing everyone's backs

November 22, 2017
Galena, Illinois

I needed a haircut, so I found a website for a "Salon & Barbershop" in Galena, which proudly proclaimed "Walk-ins welcome!" and "You are always welcome to drop in for a quick cut, just stop by anytime – during business hours, of course!" So, I did exactly that. When I got there, I saw another guy waiting. In another part of the shop, I could hear a woman doing another woman's hair (the ones I overheard for this poem). About ten minutes later an employee arrived to work, took off her coat, and greeted the guy waiting. She clearly knew him and cut his hair in about twenty minutes. He left, and the woman who cut his hair went to another part of the shop I couldn't see.

Another half hour goes by and I overhear one person say to another, "What's he doing here?"

The other woman said, "He was here when I got here."

Then a woman peers around the corner at me in the waiting area of their shop and asks, "Is there something I can help you with?"

I look around and think, *Really? They do one thing at a salon/barbershop – cut hair. What kind of question is that?* Instead, I respond, "I'm just looking to get a haircut."

She shook her head like she was dealing with someone who was clearly crazy, "No, you don't have an appointment, so you're going to have to go somewhere else. There's another salon nearby that could cut your hair."

I left without protest, despite the fact that they clearly were not busy, because I was disgusted after hearing what they were talking about. I'd rather drive 25 minutes to Dubuque to get my hair cut than give my business to a woman whose main criteria for believing a rape victim is the number of other victims who also came forward. I will not support small-mindedness (or assholes).

If Gratitude Were A Color

If gratitude
Were a color
It would glow
Like a sunset
Radiating brightly
From my soul
For all to see

> November 25, 2017
> Galena, Illinois

Thank you to Emily McDowell for posting on her Instagram the phrase, "If gratitude were a sunset."

Egg And Cheese, No Meat

On our way to the tree farm
To pick out our Christmas tree
We stopped to the local gas station
Which doubles as a pizza place
And they have breakfast sandwiches
Which is what we popped in for
I grabbed a sausage, egg, and cheese
Biscuit sandwich from the warmer
But she wanted just an egg and cheese
So we asked the people at the food counter
If they could please make one for her
The older man looked confused,
"We've got sausage, egg, and cheese
 Right there in the warmer," he said.
She said, "I just want one with no meat."
But he couldn't seem to grasp the concept
Of ordering it without the sausage.
"So, you want it without the meat?"
She replied, yes, that is what she wanted.
He turned to his co-worker and said,
"Huh. She wants a biscuit
 Egg and cheese, no meat. No meat?"
My wife nodded her head in agreement.
"No meat? No meat! So yeah,
 An egg and cheese biscuit with no meat."
After ten impossibly long minutes
His co-worker made the meatless biscuit.
After handing the hot sandwich to her,
She pulled my wife aside, pointing to a case
Filled with slices of "breakfast pizza"
And told her that some of them have no meat,
That she can order one of those next time.
Referring to a next time that will never happen
Because we will be going somewhere else

November 25, 2017
Galena, Illinois

169

We really like Casey's, but come on, really? They seriously acted like she was completely bonkers for wanting an egg and cheese breakfast sandwich.

Patriotism Is Not

Patriotism is not
How gigantic the flag is
Or how fervently it is waived
Or how many different items
Its image is affixed to.
We live in an age of idolatry
Where the symbols themselves
Are revered beyond normalcy
Instead of the actual ideals
This country was founded upon.
Its time we learn the difference
Between patriotism
And enthusiasm
Because the gulf between them
Is huge and we seem unable
To effectively differentiate
Between the two.

> November 28, 2017
> Galena, Illinois

$10,000

Today Bitcoin hit
$10,000
For the first time
Which makes me think
Back to 2010
When I first heard of it
When it was at $7
And I wonder now how
I would be spending
My millions of dollars
Had I bought it back then
When my gut instinct
Was to buy, buy, buy

November 28, 2017
Galena, Illinois

):

The Generous Dumpster

In a complete reversal
From how life's always been
In every service-related job
It seems that these days
Everyone would be
Fighting to take out the trash
Because out there, behind the store
The generous dumpster grants
The trash taker a few precious minutes
To check their phone, undisturbed

> November 28, 2017
> Galena, Illinois

When we pulled up to Casey's General Store yesterday, movement in the dumpster enclosure caught my eye. I could only make out the shoes standing in place and the edge of a jacket, but it looked like an employee standing in a weird spot…most likely checking their phone. As we were leaving, I saw a young woman with the same shoes and jacket coming around the corner, putting her phone in her pocket. I bet she jumped at the chance to take out the trash just to get a few minutes of private time to be able to check her phone.

DECEMBER

Normalcy

When our daily existence
Is consistently comprised
Of total societal dissolution
Normalcy, in any form,
Seems radically out of place
In its child-like innocence

December 1, 2017
Galena, Illinois

Watering Down

Why are fringe crazies
With easily disproven,
Stupidly-radical theories
Given a national platform
Above and beyond that of
Rational, peer-reviewed
Scientific discoveries?
Ratings.
Better ratings
Means more money.
People will line up to see
The biggest train wrecks
Spouting incredible insanity
With all parties involved
Uncaring of the ramifications
That the more susceptible
Among the population
Will glom onto the ideas,
Thinking they make sense,
Diminishing the rational
Growing the ignorant
Adding to the flood
Washing over us
From every side
Watering down
The greatness
We used to
Represent
We used to
Stand for,
But now
We sit,
And
Soon
The overwhelming tide will knock us down for good

December 1, 2017

The Cupcake

Galena, Illinois

Why does the news give airtime to flat-Earther idiots and similar fringe lunatics? That guy with the home-made rocket should have been a local paper curiosity story, not a world-wide media piece.

Despicable Diners

Out for a nice meal last night
At a nice restaurant downtown
When we overheard the words
Of the despicable diners
Seated at the next table
Discussing the recent rash
Of sexual harassment claims
Broadcast daily on the news
When one of the older men said,
"They're idiots for apologizing,
 If you don't say you're sorry
 And you keep your mouth shut
 Then as far as anyone knows
 You've done nothing wrong."
They laughed and another added,
"You're always innocent
 If you don't admit it."
They went on to call the women
Who had come forward, sluts,
While also bragging and reflecting
On all the women, the cheating,
And all things they got away with
Back when, "Things were better."
But for me
And the rest of humanity
Things will be better
Once these men
And their beliefs
Are buried deep
In the cold earth
And forgotten
Completely

                    December 7, 2017
                    Galena, Illinois

If you're the three older guys and one woman who were seated at the second table on the right wall at the Log Cabin Restaurant in Galena, Illinois last night around 7pm, you are all loathsome and a complete waste of carbon.

Think Outside The Tree

I think we might have made a mistake
When, at the Christmas tree farm,
We decided to think outside the tree
And opt instead for a festive wreath
A huge one, four feet in diameter
That we wrapped in lights
And hung above the couch
Which, at first glance
Is something different
And a fresh new idea
But now, two weeks in,
We're rethinking the notion
As needles now rain on us
When we sit down or stand up
And we now have a new ritual
Of vacuuming the couch
First thing every morning
Making this even worse
Than that one year
Where our "tree"
Was a camera tripod
Wrapped in several strings
Of blinking, colorful lights

December 7, 2017
Galena, Illinois

Maybe not worse, but this wreath is definitely a lot messier.

Knowing The Potential

Spiritual aftershocks
From deeply meditating –
Energy driving, leaping,
Reverberating through me
Quickening my heart
Quaking across my arms
Striking like lightning
When my mind returns
Thinking about the things
I was intensely focusing on
Leaving me disheveled
And out of sorts for hours
Unable to see everyday life
In the same mundane way
Knowing the potential
That exists within us,
Each and every one of us,
And what we are capable of

December 17, 2017
Galena, Illinois

Suitcases Of Beer

As I pulled in and parked
At the local convenience store
In the early afternoon
I saw not one, not two,
But three men exiting,
All separately,
All dutifully carrying
Their daily assignment
What appeared to be
Suitcases of beer,
To their trucks,
Heading home
From their day job
They get paid for
Going home
To get to work
On their night job
They pay for

December 20, 2017
Galena, Illinois

Just Like That

We were watching Netflix
When our Internet connection
Just stopped working
And stayed stopped
After half an hour
Of hoping it would start again
And then resetting the router
I called the provider's number
For their tech support department
Where, for the next 20 minutes,
I defensively answered questions
All implying we were the ones
Who must have done something
To sabotage our own connection
And then, for no reason,
It started working, just like that
After we were done talking
And I was thinking how
The guy talked down to me,
In tone and implication,
That if there were another option
For Internet in this little town
I would switch, just like that

December 23, 2017
Galena, Illinois

A very real requirement for future places we're going to live is
Mediacom cannot be the sole Internet provider. If so, we will not
live there.

The Land Is Quiet

Late afternoon drive
On a country back road
Looking across
The endless fields
The land is quiet
Steeped in the midst
Of it's midwinter sleep
After three seasons
Of working and giving
With the gray ceiling
Mirroring the nothing
Surrounding me for miles

December 23, 2017
Galena, Illinois

Once or twice a week, we like to take "the long way" when we go to Casey's to get a fountain drink. When we went the other day, looking out over the miles of barren fields that were full of corn a few months ago, it struck me how quiet the land was.

I Wouldn't Understand

Walking the dogs in our yard
When the sound of a vehicle
Going two to three times
The posted speed limit
Clearly oblivious of the
Very sharp corner ahead
Clearly not caring one bit
Considering the addition
Of the parallel sound
The end-over-end clanking
Of hollow aluminum on asphalt
Signaling that the jeep
Roaring on by had just
Ejected some refuse
In the form of a beer can
Coming to rest in the road
But apparently it's ok
That I didn't know why
Someone would act like this
Because as the windshield sticker
Smugly told me, "It's a Jeep thing,"
So I wouldn't understand

          December 23, 2017
          Galena, Illinois

Actually, I *do* understand. You're just a shitty person.

Powdered Sugar

The billowing bags above
Light and locked together
Like a winter's puffy coat
Tinged a dozen ways of gray
Slowly sifting the contents
Across anything horizontal
Painting the landscape
Like a carnival food cart
Dusts the fried dough
With powdered sugar
Flavoring the season
To match the expectations

December 24, 2017
Galena, Illinois

We got about an inch of snow and everything looked like it was decorated with powdered sugar.

Window Shopping

Christmas Eve
In a little town
Depending on
Tourist dollars
But as we drove
Down Main St.
We saw people
Lots of people
Filling sidewalks
Window shopping
And that's it
Because 90%
Of the stores
Were closed
For the holiday,
But the tourists
Are right here
Money in hand
Wanting to see
Wanting to spend
And will instead
Be leaving here
With the bad taste
Of being denied
The experience
They came for

December 24, 2017
Galena, Illinois

Seriously? Come on, Galena. At 2pm today we drove down Main Street and there were *hundreds* of people walking and window shopping because maybe only 5% of the shops were open. When you work in a location that depends on tourism, you need to adjust your schedule to adapt to their needs.

December

After three or four lines I noticed the lines were all about the same length so I tried to keep that going for the entire poem.

In Flyover Country

In flyover country
Looking up
At the planes
Flying over, way overhead
From somewhere
(Never here)
To somewhere else
(Also, never here)
Wondering who
Those people are,
Wondering where
They come from, and
Where they're going

December 26, 2017
Galena, Illinois

No matter the hour, every time I'm outside and I look up, there's a plane in the sky going right or left.

A Cold So Deep

A cold so deep
Tightly gripping
Shortening the breath
Stealing the warmth
Quickening the steps
Moving you along
Guiding you inside
Back where you belong

> December 26, 2017
> Galena, Illinois

The dogs are very unhappy with these below zero temperatures.

As a side note, it takes me a lot longer to write shorter poems. I wrote, re-wrote, edited, deleted, and re-wrote this one for longer than I'd like to admit.

I Am Not Concerned

I am not concerned
About the news stories
Screaming in my face
Because most of that
Has little to no bearing
On the normal and
Everyday lives that
You or I spend our
Precious time living
I am not bothered by
The repeated attempts
To get me riled up
Because I can think
For myself and choose
To use my critical
Reasoning skills
As I look at who
Is telling me this thing
Who is paying for it
And what are they
Trying to sell to me
It may be a product
It may be an idea
Or it may be both
I am not going to
Let myself be swayed
By people or groups
Looking to dupe me
Into believing anything
That has not suffered
Through the repeated
Burning furnace crucible
Of peer-reviewed
Science-based scrutiny
Everything else
Is just ignored
And disregarded

December

As background noise

December 26, 2017
Galena, Illinois

I was listening to "Anna Begins" by Counting Crows and the line, "I am not overly concerned," stuck in my head and I started writing something based on that phrase.

Squeaky Crunching

Stepping out, outside
Into the white-covered landscape
With each step sinking down slightly
Forever damaging the powderous mat
With the squeaky crunching sound
Signaling my approach
And the set of footprints
Showing my direction

December 31, 2017
Galena, Illinois

Ha! When writing the date, I inadvertently wrote "2018." I guess
I'm ready for the new year.

December

The Cupcake

IF YOU ENJOYED THIS COLLECTION

Please consider rating it at Amazon.com. As an independent author, having people review my works is critical in helping to increase my exposure and letting new people discover books like this. Thank you!

WRITTEN BY ERIC NIXON

The Cupcake – 2017 poetry collection
2492: Attack Of The Ancient Cyborg – science fiction novel
The Ocean Above – 2016 poetry collection
Cascadia's Fault – 2015 poetry collection
The Taborist – 2014 poetry collection
The Entire Universe – 2013 poetry collection
Trying Not To Blink – 2012 poetry collection
Lost In Thought – poetry collection
Emily Dickinson – Superhero: Vol. 1 – historical fiction novel
Incident On The Hennepin – a short story set in *2492*
Plenty Of Time – a short story
Retribution On A Jetpack – a short story set in *2492*
Anything But Dreams – poetry collection

Available at Amazon.com/author/ericnixon

ABOUT THE AUTHOR

Eric Nixon is a poet and author who has written eight collections of poetry, several short stories, and a two novels, *2492: Attack Of The Ancient Cyborg* and *Emily Dickinson, Superhero – Vol. 1*. Eric lives with his author wife, Kari Chapin, in the Midwest.

The Cupcake

www.ingramcontent.com/pod-product-compliance
Lightning Source LLC
Chambersburg PA
CBHW060834110426
R18122100001BA/R181221PG42736CBX00029BA/31

* 9 780099 843 6227 *